D1527394

FROM THE GREEK ANTHOLOGY

FROM THE
GREEK ANTHOLOGY

Poems in English Paraphrase

DUDLEY FITTS (1903-)

FABER AND FABER

24 Russell Square

London

First published in England in mcmlvii
by Faber and Faber Limited
24 Russell Square London W.C.1.
Printed in Great Britain
at the Bowering Press Plymouth

CONTENTS

*The numerals following the titles refer to the various Books of the
Greek Anthology. In the few cases where poems are drawn from
other sources, the reference is to Mackail's Select Epigrams from
the Greek Anthology [London: 1911. 3rd edition].*

5

7

9

10

[1938]

The Greek, or 'Palatine', Anthology, together with the so-called *Appendix Planudeana*, contains rather more than four thousand epigrams, pagan and Christian, and represents a period of approximately seventeen hundred years, beginning in 700 B.C. In spite of the limiting characteristics of the form itself (brevity, a certain stylization of diction, the general preponderance of the elegiac couplet), this vast collection is marked by a variety as inexhaustible as that of the shifting civilizations that it mirrors. The range of subject-matter is immense: the same form expresses the magnificent epitaphs of Simonidês, the dyspeptic didacticisms of Palladas, the half-oriental luxuriance of Meleagros' lyrics, the bawdy lampoons of Lucilius, and the sterile classroom exercises of those forgotten rhetoricians who liked to set themselves such problems as *What Alkêstis might have said when Admêtos yoked to his chariot a Lion and a Boar,*[1] or *What Love would say if he were to fall in love.*[2] The varying degrees of artistic merit are no less strongly marked. Certain of the elegies attributed to Plato, for instance, or the epigrams of Kallimachos at his best, are for ever and fatally beyond the scope of any translator. At the other end of the scale is the tedious doggerel of the Imperial riffraff and the Byzantine monks. And all the world lies between.

It is a curious thing that of all this material there is scarcely a single adequate translation into English verse. Many have tried—or, in Mr. Shane Leslie's somewhat

[1] IX:466   [2] IX:449

Alexandrian phrase, 'Many a silver pitcher has been lowered by many a purple cord into these gathered fountains of Hellas'; but the results have seldom been happy. Even Shelley's *Thou wert the morning star* is sorry stuff when one compares it with that miraculous original, which Mackail calls 'perhaps the most perfect epigram ever written in any language':

> Ἀστὴρ πρὶν μὲν ἔλαμπες ἐνὶ ζωοῖσιν Ἐῷος·
> νῦν δὲ θανὼν λάμπεις Ἕσπερος ἐν φθιμένοις.[1]

and I must confess that I have never been able to understand the praise generally awarded William Johnson Cory's version of Kallimachos' famous elegy:

They told me, Heraclitus, they told me you were dead. [2]

Indeed, this particular jingle seems to me to illustrate admirably what so often happens to a translator when he undertakes one of the epigrams. Possibly it is the fault of the elegiac couplet itself: the dactylic rhythm is deceptive and beguiling, and the form's extreme concentration, suggesting immediately a pair of dainty quatrains or, worse, the neo-Swinburnian canter, very easily results in triviality. Whatever the reason, too many of the English translations are little more than competent *vers de société*: the plangent cadences of the Greek have gone over into something awkwardly reminiscent of a Savoy Opera patter-song. It is significant, too, that this same *reductio ad pistrinam* impairs, though less seriously, the ordinary translations of Horace.

In making this collection from the *Anthology* I have been restrained by a most angelic fear of treading. In the first

---

[1] VII:670. Ascribed to Plato.   [2] VII:80. Cf. p. 70 *infra*.

place, I have not presumed to touch the greatest of the epigrams: they are not within my range. In the second place, I have avoided (partly for the reasons I have suggested above) regularity of stanza form and rime. I find it impossible to equal the delicate balance of the elegiac couplet, and I have deliberately chosen a system of irregular cadence, assonance, and the broken line. And finally, I have not really undertaken translation at all—translation, that is to say, as it is understood in the schools. I have simply tried to restate in my own idiom what the Greek verses have meant to me. The disadvantages of this method are obvious: it has involved cutting, altering, expansion, revision—in short, all the devices of free paraphrase. Occasionally, as in the treatment of some of the lampoons, my attempt to preserve the spirit has resulted in a scandalous departure from the letter; but only once or twice, I think, have I been consciously perverse—in my version of Eratosthenês' Pooh-bah lines on Virginity,[1] for instance, where I have employed a stuffy diction and a costive technic to suggest the arid pedantic quality of the original. (And maybe even this is legitimate: for while it is certain that Eratosthenês was not trying to make so lugubrious a noise, it is equally certain that that is precisely the kind of noise that he managed to make.) In general, my purpose has been to compose first of all, and as simply as possible, an English poem. To this end I have discarded poeticisms, even where (as in Meleagros, for instance) they could have been defended. Except in certain Dedications and in similar pieces where the language is definitely liturgical, I have avoided such archaisms as 'thou' and 'ye' and all their train of attendant ghosts. Less defens-

[1] *Infra*, p. 38. For the Greek, cf. IX:444.

ibly, I have risked a spurious atmosphere of monotheism by writing 'God' for 'Zeus' (but Mr. Leslie would have it 'Jupiter'!) whenever the context admitted it without too perilous a clash. And for my use of the direct rather than the Latin transliteration of proper names I can plead only that my reasons are so entirely subjective that they are beyond useful debate.

The best translations of the epigrams are in prose, and at least two of these are excellent. Professor Mackail's *Select Epigrams*,[1] with its invaluable preface and notes, is a *liber aureus*, unsurpassed of its kind. The translations are sensitive, graceful, and admirably successful in recreating the original moods; I can think of no finer introduction to the *Anthology*, whatever the extent of the reader's Greek. Shane Leslie's *The Greek Anthology*[2] contains more than a thousand of the epigrams; it is urbane and witty, and there is an entertaining and informative *Prolegomenon*. It is not, however, to be classed with Mackail's book. Finally, for the student who must have the entire *Anthology* there are five volumes of the Loeb Classical Library,[3] with the Greek text, and a literal translation by W. R. Paton.

D F

Biddeford Pool

[1] J. W. Mackail: *Select Epigrams from the Greek Anthology*. London: Longmans Green, and Co. 1911 (*3rd edition.*)

[2] Shane Leslie: *The Greek Anthology*. London: Ernest Benn Ltd. 1929.

[3] W. R. Paton: *The Greek Anthology*. London: William Heinemann (Cambridge: Harvard University Press). 1916-26. 5 vols.

NOTE

[1956]

In collecting and reissuing these poems, I have decided to
let the greater number of them stand in the form in which
they were first published. My theories of translation have
changed so radically that any attempt to recast the work of
fifteen or twenty years ago could end only in confusion and
the stultification of whatever force the poems may once
have had; accordingly, I have contented myself with cor-
recting only such errors as were the result of my ignorance
or of inconsistencies in my method.

D F

LECTORI SALUTEM

Reader, here is no Priam
Slain at the altar,
    here are no fine tales
Of Medêa, of weeping Niobê,
      here you will find
No mention of Itys in his chamber
And never a word about nightingales in the trees.

Earlier poets have left full accounts of these matters.

I sing of Love and the Graces, I sing of Wine:
What have they in common with Tragedy's cosmic scowl?

PRIAPOS OF THE HARBOUR

Now Spring returning beckons the little boats
Once more to dance on the waters: the grey storms
Are gone that scourged the sea. Now swallows build
Their round nests in the rafters, and all the fields
Are bright with laughing green.
      Come then, my sailors:
Loose your dripping hawsers, from their deep-sunk graves
Haul up your anchors, raise your brave new sails.

It is Priapos warns you, god of this harbour.

PAN AND THE NYMPHS

'O Nymphs, did Daphnis, passing by,
Stop here to rest with his shaggy white goats?
Tell me truly.'
                    'Yes, yes, piper Pan,
And there on the poplar's bark he carved for you
A letter saying *O Pan, Pan, come!*
Come to Maleia, to the mount of Psôphis:
I shall wait for you there.'
                            'Goodbye, dear Nymphs: I go.'

COLD PASTORAL

Homeward at evening through the drifted snow
The cows plod back to shelter from the hill;
But ah, the long strange sleep
Of the cow-herd Therimachos lying beneath the oak,
Struck still, still, by the fire that falls from heaven!

INSCRIPTION FOR A STATUE OF PAN

Be still O green cliffs of the Dryads
Still O springs bubbling from the rock
                                        and be still
Manyvoiced cry of the ewes:
                              It is Pan
Pan with his tender pipe:
                            the clever lips run
Over the withied reeds
                        while all about him
Rise up from the ground to dance with joyous tread
The Nymphs of the Water
                          Nymphs of the Oaken Forest

ALPHEIOS OF MITYLENE

PRAYER TO POSEIDON

Governor of swift ships, Master of horses,
Ruler of the sheer down-thrusting crag of Euboia,
Grant us, Poseidôn, safe passage
From our Syrian docks to the harbour of Arês' town.

ON TROY FALLEN

O City, where are the once proud walls, the temples
Heavy with riches? Where are the sacred heads
Of oxen slain at the altars? Where
Are the Paphian's precious jars and her golden cloak?
Where is the image of your own Athenê?

Gone, gone, lost to War and Time,
And to bleak Fate, reverser of happy fortunes,
And to harsh Envy.
                    But the name of Troy
And the glory of Troy shall live to see these die.

ARCHIAS THE MACEDONIAN

HEKTOR OF TROY

Stone, who was his father that lies beneath you?
What was his name? His country? What was his death?

His father was Priam. Ilion his country. His name
Was Hektor. He met death fighting for his land.

DEDICATION OF A BOW: TO SERAPIS

Menoitas of Lyktos dedicates thus his bow:

O Serapis, thine are the bow of horn and the quiver.
The quiver is empty.
                    The enemy has my arrows.

PARMENION

ON THE DEAD AT THERMOPYLAI

Him who, altering the ways of earth and sea,
Sailed on the land and made his march on the water,
Him the valour of three hundred Spartan spears hurled back.

Be ashamed O mountains and sea!

ANAKREON

EPITAPH

Here lies Timokritos: soldier: valiant in battle.
Arês spares not the brave man, but the coward.

DEDICATION OF A LANCE

Idle now in Athenê's shining house,
Brass tip no longer red with enemy blood,
Stand, lance of Echekratidas,

                      a witness
To all men that this soldier of Crete was brave.

ANTIPHILOS OF BYZANTIUM

IMAGINARY DIALOGUE

This cloak of purple, Leonidas, Xerxês gives you
Praising your courage in battle.

                      Let Xerxês keep
His gift for traitors. Cover me with my shield:
I want no richer burial.

                      But you are dead.
Must you hate the Persians even when you are dead?
Soldier, the love of freedom can not die.

DEDICATION OF A TRAGIC MASK
TO THE MUSES

Praying for learning
                    Simos the son of Mikkos
Dedicates me to the Muses: they in return
For a small gift granting a great.
                                And so I lean
Yawning against this Samian *Y* on the schoolroom wall
A Dionysos of Tragedy
                        hearing the little boys
Recite *My hair is holy*:
                    'telling me my own dream'.

DEDICATION: TO PAN

His pierced shepherd-pipe,
His hairy mantle, his club,
Daphnis the lover of women
                        now dedicates to his dear Pan.
O Pan, receive these gifts of Daphnis:
For like him you love music,
                        like him you are luckless in love.

AGATHIAS

THE SWALLOWS

But all my night has been sleepless! And now, at dawn,
You chattering swallows bring tears to my eyes again
And sweet rest flies from me. Sightless I stare,
But still Rhodanthê lingers in my heart.

Oh be still, you twittering gossips! Was it I
Cut out Philomela's tongue?
                      Be off to the hills,
Go, perch by the hoopoe's nest among the crags
And mourn your Itylos there—
                            but let me sleep,
That for a little space some wandering dream
May come and lock Rhodanthê's arms about me.

PLATO

DEDICATION OF A MIRROR

I Laïs whose laughter was scornful in Hellas,
Whose doorways were thronged daily with young lovers,
I dedicate my mirror to Aphroditê:

For I will not see myself as I am now,
And can not see myself as once I was.

24

EPITAPH OF THE SINGING-GIRL MUSA

Musa the blue-eyed, the sweetly singing nightingale,
Lies here suddenly mute in this little grave,
Still as a stone, who was once so witty, so much loved:

Pretty Musa, may this dust rest lightly upon you.

ANONYMOUS

EPITAPH OF A GIRL

The monument of Phrasikleia:

For ever shall I be called virgin,
The gods having granted me this instead of marriage.

MELEAGROS

HER VOICE

I swear it, by Love I swear it!

More sweet to me is Hêliodôra's voice
Than the holy harp of Lêto's golden Son.

TO HELIODORA

Fill the cup, and again cry, again, again,
Héliodôra!
Speak, and with that sweet name alone
Temper the wine. And bring me (what though it be
yesterday's?)
The garland drenched in her perfume, that I may put on
Her memory.
       See, how the Rose of Love is weeping
Because it knows she is elsewhere, not in my arms!

MELEAGROS

THE NIGHT ALONE

O Night, O sleepless tossing, longing for Hêliodôra!
Poor eyes hot with tears in the lingering white dawn!
Is she lonely too? Is she dreaming of how I kissed her,
And dreaming so, does she turn to kiss the dream of me?
      —or a new love? a newer toy?

Forbid it, lamp!
See it never!
Did I not set you to guard her?

TO THE MORNING STAR

O Morning Star thou enemy of Love!

How lazily dost thou creep 'round the world tonight,
This night, while another lies warm beneath her cloak!
But when she lay, my slim love, in these arms,
Then didst thou come—how quickly O Star!—to stand
    over us,
Drenching us in thy light that laughed at our loss,

O morning Star, thou enemy of Love!

A LOVER'S CURSE

This thing I pray, dearest Night, Mother of all the gods:
This thing only I pray, holy propitious Night:

If another man lies with her now: if another,
Close-clasped beneath her cloak, is touching her—
Hêliodôra, Hêliodôra, the sweet despair of sleep—

Then let the light go out!
                Let his
Heavy eyes fail him!
                  Let him fall asleep
Locked in her arms, a second Endymiôn!

AGAINST MOSQUITOES

Squealshrilling Mosquitoes, fraternity lost to shame,
Obscene vampires, chittering riders of the night:
Let her sleep, I beg you!, and come
(If you must come) feed on this flesh of mine.

(Oh useless prayer! Must not her body charm
The wildest, most heartless, most insensate beasts?)

Yet hear me, devils, I have warned you:
                              No more of your daring,
Or you shall smart from the strength of my jealous hands!

THE MOSQUITO

Fly to her, swiftly fly, Mosquito, bearing my greeting:
Perch on the tip of her ear, and whisper it to her:
Say *He lies waking, longing for you: and you, sleeping,*
Sleeping, O shameless girl!, have never a thought for who loves
    you!
Buzz!
     Chirr!
           Off to her, sweetest Musician!
Yet speak to her softly, lest
Her bedfellow wake and hurt her because of my love.

. . . or bring me the girl herself, Mosquito, and I
Will crown your head with the lion's mane and give you
Strong Heraklês' bludgeon to brandish in your paw.

FLOWERS: FOR HELIODORA

White violets I'll bring
And soft narcissus
And myrtle and laughing lilies
The innocent crocus
Dark hyacinth also
And roses heavy with love

And these I'll twine for Hêliodôra
And scatter the bright petals on her hair.

MELEAGROS

HELIODORA'S FINGERNAIL

O Fingernail of Hêliodôra,
Surely Love sharpened you, surely Love made you grow:
Does not your lightest touch transfix my heart?

LULLABY

Sleep sleep dear girl, drowsy flower:

Ah that I were the Lord of Sleep, that so,
Wingless, a whisper,
Under your shadowy eyelids I might creep:

Then, not even he who veils God's eyes
Could come in to you:
                              you would be mine alone.

REDIMICULUM PUELLARUM

O Love, by Timo's curls,
                              by Hêliodôra's sandal,
By Demo's myrrhdrenched threshold,
                              by Antikleia's slow smile,
By the dear flowers twined in Dorotheia's hair—
O Love, Love, I swear
Your quiver is empty:
                    all your shafts
Have fled unswerving to bury themselves in my heart.

THE FLOWER-GIRL

Rose-girl, rose of a girl, tell me:
What will you sell me?
Your roses?
             Yourself?
                        Or both?

MARCUS ARGENTARIUS

HESIOD,
FORTUNATE DELIVERANCE FROM

Lately thumbing the pages of *Works and Days*,
I saw my Pyrrhê coming.
                Goodbye book!
'Why in the world should I cobweb my days,' I cried,
'With the works of Old Man Hesiod?'

PLATO

THE APPLE

I am an apple tossed by one who loves you.
Yield to him therefore, dear Xanthippê:
                        both you and I decay.

31

'NOT OF ITSELF, BUT THEE'

Perfume sweet I send you,
                    gracing not you but the perfume:
You are yourself the perfume of the perfume.

ASKLEPIADES

TO HIS MISTRESS

You deny me: and to what end?
There are no lovers, dear, in the under world,
No love but here: only the living know
The sweetness of Aphroditê—
                    but below,
But in Acherôn, careful virgin, dust and ashes
Will be our only lying down together.

RUFINUS DOMESTICUS

TO MELITE

Melitê, your eyes are Hêra's,
                your hands are Athenê's, Melitê,
Aphroditê's your breasts,
                and your feet are the feet of Thetis.

I called him blessed who looks on you, and thrice blessed
Who hears your voice; and he is a demigod
Who kisses your mouth:
                but a god, a god indeed
Is the man whose bed receives you as his bride!

AGATHIAS

DIALOGUE

A: Why that alarming sigh? *B*: I'm in love.
A: With a boy or a girl? *B*: With a girl.
A: Attractive? *B*: *I* think so!
A: Where did you meet her?
B: Last night at a dinner-party.
A: I see. And you think you've a chance with her?
B: I'm sure of it; but
    It's got to be kept a secret, friend.
A: Ah. Then you mean
    That you are not contemplating Holy Matrimony?
B: That isn't it. I mean
    That I've learned she hasn't a penny in the world.
A: You've 'learned'!—
    Liar, liar, you're not in love!
    The heart struck silly by Love's shaft
    Forgets its arithmetic!

C   *33*

ON KALLISTION THE COURTESAN

O thou of Kypros:
Thou of Kythêra: of Milêtos:
Thou Aphroditê of the beautiful Syrian plains
And plunging horses:

Be gracious to Kallistion
                  who has never
Barred her door in the face of a lover.

WITH A GARLAND, TO RHODOKLEIA

This garland, Rhodokleia, I myself
Made, with my own hands twining the fair flowers:
Here are lilies, cupped roses, anemone
Weeping, the soft narcissus, dark violets.
                                Take them,
Wear them, but do not be proud:
The garland must wither at last, and you will fade.

THE SWEETNESS OF LOVE

Sweet in summer is snow to thirsty lips,
Sweet to sailors' eyes the Northern Crown
Bringing back Spring:
      but sweeter far
When two in love lie close beneath one cloak
Honouring Kypris.

KALLIMACHOS

ZEUS THE LOVER

Hate him O Zeus if he hates me—
Theokritos, my Theokritos, deliciously bronzed—
Hate the boy four times as much as he hates me!

Heavenly Zeus, by Ganymede I swear,
The goldenhaired,
You in your time have loved.
          I say no more.

MANIFESTO

Let Aphroditê herself,
     let all the company of Love
Curse me, shrivel my sick heart with their hate, if ever
I turn to the love of boys.
     O Goddess,
From sliding error and perversion guard me!
To sin with girls is sin enough:
Pittalakos may have the rest.

COMPLEYNT

Tired of life, and not yet twenty-two!

Little Devils of Love, your fury! your stinging!
Must you torment me so?
     And when you have done for me,
What then? Why then, I suppose,
Back to your infantile dicing, as before!

SOKRATES TO AGATHON

My soul, when I kissed Agathôn, crept up to my lips
As though it wished (poor thing!) to cross over to him.

THE LOST BRIDE

At the bridal bed of star-crossed Petalê
Hadês, not Hymen, stood:
                              for as she fled
Alone through the night, dreading Love's first stroke
(As virgins will), the brutal watch-dogs seized her.

And we, whose morning hope had been a wife,
Found scarce enough of her body for burial.

PALLADAS

COUPLET

To the man who has married an ugly wife
Lamp-light's an even deeper darkness.

ERATOSTHENES SCHOLASTIKOS

MEDITATION, FOLLOWED BY
EXCELLENT ADVICE

How delectable are the attributes of Virginity!
Nevertheless it is clear
That general virginity would annihilate the Race.

Marriage, therefore, would seem the more practical plan:
Marry, and contrive a man
Who, when you have ceased to exist, will take your place.

Eschew, nevertheless, lechery.

MARCUS ARGENTARIUS

'RUMORESQUE SENUM SEVERIORUM'

It was this way:

I'd been going for weeks with this girl,
Alkippê her name was; well, so
One night I manage to get her up to my room.
That's all right,
Though our hearts are cloppety-clopping like mad
For fear we'll be caught together.
                                    Well,
Everything's fine, you know what I mean, when
All of a sudden the door pops
And in pokes her old mother's sheep-head:
'Remember, daughter,' she bleats, 'you and I go halves!'

38

BRIEF AUTUMNAL

Green grape, and you refused me.
  Ripe grape, and you sent me packing.
    Must you deny me a bite of your raisin?

GIRL BETRAYED

With the treason of mingled love and wine
Nikagoras lulled her to sleep,
                    and now
To Aphroditê Aglaonikê dedicates
The myrrh-wet spoils of her innocence:
The sandals, and the light zone
That bound her breasts:
                    to bear witness
That she was sleeping and he was merciless.

EOTHEN

Fair are the boys of Tyre, by Love I swear it!
But Myiskos
Sweeps the bright stars from the sky, that bursting sun.

AGATHIAS

KALLIRRHOE: A DEDICATION

To Aphroditê these wreaths
To Athenê this lock of my hair
To Artemis my girdle:

I Kallirrhoê
Brought to my virgin bed a valiant husband
And bore him men.

MELEAGROS

THE WINE-CUP

This cup has touched
Zenophila's teasing mouth, sweet snare of love.
Oh happiness, if she
Would press her lips to my lips, and in one
Deep draught drink down my soul!

TANTALOS

Mouth to mouth joined we lie, her naked breasts
Curved to my fingers, my fury grazing deep
On the silver plain of her throat,
                              and then: no more.
She denies me her bed. Half of her body to Love
She has given, half to Prudence:
                              I die between.

ANONYMOUS

THE SERENADER

Boy, hold my wreath for me.

The night is black,
                    the path is long,
And I am completely and beautifully drunk.
Nevertheless I will go
To Themison's house and sing beneath his window.
You need not come with me:
                              though I may stumble,
He is a steady lamp for the feet of love.

PHILODEMOS THE EPICUREAN

REMONSTRANCE

So I am your 'darling girl'!
                    Your tears
Say so, and the sleights your hands play,
You are conventionally jealous, and your kisses
Suggest a lover who knows just what he wants.

I am the more confused, then,
For when I whisper 'Here I am, take me, come,'
You fuss, cough, and adjourn the session *sine die*.

Are you a Lover or a Senator?

RUFINUS

'AUT NEUTRUM . . . VEL DUOS'

O Love, bringer of fire,
If you can not kindle both of us equally,
Quench or transfer the consuming flame of one.

A WHORE'S BED OF LAUREL

The fugitive from the bed of one
A bed for many has become.

ANDANTE, MA NON ASSAI

If girls were as charming after the fact as before it,
What man would ever tire?
But the sad truth is,
Just then the dearest of wives is a joyless problem.

TO ZEUS OF THE RAINS

Rain at night and the north wind whirling
And wine and the stumbling loneliness:
Moschos my fair love!
I cried . . .

> (Trudge on, on, and never a friendly door
> Down all the long street . . .)

I cried
Dripping with rain:
No end, O Zeus?
Dear Zeus, be gentle! Were you not once in love?

INSCRIPTION FOR A PAINTING

This is Eurotas, the Lakonian river, and this
Is Lêda, nearly naked, and the Swan you see
Conceals great Zeus.
          O little Loves,
You that lead me so unwillingly to love,
What bird can I be?
          If Zeus is a Swan,
I must be, I suppose, a Goose.

HERMIONE'S GIRDLE

Aphroditê, dear Goddess:
Once I was playing with lovely Hermionê,
And about her waist, O Paphian Queen, she wore
A girdle wrought with letters of gold:
          LOVE ME
AND BE NOT ANGRY IF I BELONG TO ANOTHER.

DEDICATION OF A LAMP: TO SERAPIS

Her precious lamp with its twenty flaming wicks
To thee O Serapis God of Kanôpos
Kallistion daughter of Kritias dedicates:

This was the vow she made for her child Apellis:

But thou O God: look on my glory
                      and thou shalt cry
O Evening Star how art thou fallen from Heaven!

DIOPHANES OF MYRINA

ON LOVE

Love's thrice a robber, however you take it:
    He's desperate,
               sleepless,
                    and he strips us naked.

PRAISE OF WOMEN

Only twice is womankind
Anything but an affliction:

(1) in bride-bed
&
(2) in the grave.

DANAE

As a golden rain you embraced Danaê, O Zeus,
That the girl might yield to the gift, not cringe from the god.

THE VINE AND THE GOAT

Gnaw me down to the ground, O Goat:
Nevertheless my fruit shall survive
To make libation at your sacrifice.

46

STATEMENT

And this I say though, hearing, they believe me not:
I say that my hand has fixed the limit of this art,
And (though no mortal work can exist without flaw)
This my mark is established for ever and will not be passed.

LUCILIUS

A VALENTINE FOR A LADY

Darling, at the Beautician's you buy
Your (a) hair
     (b) complexion
     (c) lips
     (d) dimples, &
     (e) teeth.
For a like amount you could just as well buy a face.

ANONYMOUS

EPITAPH OF DIONYSIOS OF TARSOS

At sixty I, Dionysios of Tarsos, lie here,
Never having married:
               and I wish my father had not.

47

PALLADAS

ON MEMPHIS THE DANCER

As Daphnê and Niobê, pugnosed Memphis
Dances the dance of stock and stone.

AMMONIDES

SECRET WEAPON

Send Antipatra naked to meet the Parthian cavalry,
And the Parthian cavalry
Will stampede at once beyond the last horizon.

LUCILIUS

THE SLENDER MAIDEN

When as in sleep Artemidôra lay,
Demetrios fanned her with an ostrich-plume, &
Blew her clean out of the house.

ON MARCUS THE PHYSICIAN

Yesterday Dr Marcus went to see the statue of Zeus.
Though Zeus,
              & though marble,
We're burying the statue today.

ON SOBER AKINDYNOS

We were all drunk but Akindynos
And so Akindynos
Seemed the only drunkard of us all.

ON ENVIOUS DIOPHON

Diophôn was crucified:
But, seeing beside him another on a loftier cross,
He died of envy.

THE FRUGAL HOST

My dinner yesterday was the shin of an elderly goat
And a serving of hempen cabbage ten days cut.
My host's name? I'll not tell you:
He's an irritable chap, and might invite me again!

ON MAUROS THE RHETOR

Lo, I beheld Mauros,
Professor of Public Speaking,
Raise high his elephant-snout
And from between his lips
(12 oz. apiece) give vent
To a voice whose very sound is accomplished murder.

I was impressed.

ON A FORTUNE-TELLER

Firmly, as with one voice,
The entire Faculty of the College of Applied Astrology
Foretold a healthy old age for my father's brother.

Hermokleidês alone
Maintained that he would die young:
                    but he made this statement
At the funeral service we held for my father's brother.

TO A FRIEND:
CONSTRUCTIVE CRITICISM

Lift sunward yr considerable nose,
                    fling wide th'abyss of yr mouth,
And you'll make a presentable sun-dial for all who pass by.

ON TORPID MARCUS

Lazy Marcus once dreamed he was running a race.
    (N.B.: He never went to bed again.)

ANONYMOUS

ON A SCHOOL-TEACHER

Hail O ye seven pupils
Of Aristeidês the Rhetorician:

4 walls
& 3 settees.

ERATOSTHENES SCHOLASTIKOS

DEDICATION OF A WINE-JUG

To thee, O Bacchos, Xenophôn the drinker of wine
Dedicates this empty jug.
                    Accept it graciously.
                    It is all he owns.

NIKARCHOS

VALENTINE FOR A POPULAR TENOR

Fatal, fatal is the song of the dire night-raven:
But when Demophilos sings
Even the dire night-raven blenches & dies.

ON HERMOGENES THE PHYSICIAN

Diophantos went to bed
              & dreamed of Dr Hermogenês.

Although he was wearing a Lucky Piece,
              he never woke up again.

LUCIAN OF SAMOSATA

MEDITATION ON BEAVERS

O lovely Whiskers O inspirational Mop!
But if growing a beard, my friend, means acquiring wisdom,
Any old goat can be Plato.

LUCILIUS

ON ADRASTOS THE RHETORICIAN

Wheezing into the saddle of a winged ant,
Adrastos, Professor of Beautiful Literature,
Cleared his throat & spake:
Fly forth, O Pégasos mine!
              Now hast thou thy Bellerophon!

Ay, truly: that he has—
A half-dead skull-&-bones.

COMPLAINT

I adore you darling,
                    I love everything about you:
Only, dearest, I deplore that glad eye of yours
So easily pleased with all manner of loathly Collegians.

DIOGENES LAERTIUS

TAUROMANCY AT MEMPHIS

At Memphis the horn'd bull told our friend
Eudoxos of his approaching end.
That is the story I have heard.
But lest you think me so absurd
As to believe that bulls can chatter,
Or bull-calves either, for that matter,
Hear what happened: the prophetic brute
With its long wet tongue lapped the fine new suit
Eudoxos was wearing, as much as to say
Your demise is arranged for this very day.
Whereat our friend obligingly
Went home & died. Age? 53.

ON APIS THE PRIZEFIGHTER

TO APIS THE BOXER
HIS GRATEFUL OPPONENTS HAVE ERECTED
THIS STATUE
HONOURING HIM
WHO NEVER BY ANY CHANCE HURT ONE OF THEM

NIKARCHOS

FORTUNATUS THE R.A.

Fortunatus the portrait-painter got twenty sons
But never one likeness.

ANONYMOUS

EPITAPH OF A NICENE ACTOR

Philistion of Nikaia lies here, whose laughter
Lightened the heavy lives of his fellow men;
And with him all life lies,
               who died
Often, indeed, but never quite in this fashion.

55

ON KRITON THE MISER

To ease his rumbling stomach our Kritôn sniffs
Not mint,
But the product of the Mint.

LEONIDAS THE ALEXANDRIAN

COMPENSATION

Simylos the harper played a night-long recital,
And of all the neighbourhood only old Origen lived,
For he was deaf:

        and the gods, in their merciful wisdom,
Had granted him length of days in place of hearing.

THE TIMID VETERAN

Calpurnius, our favourite *miles gloriosus*,
Strayed into an art gallery, and there
Ran into a mural of the Trojan War.

He goggled
                swooned
                        crying *I yield*,
O comrade Trojans, belov'd of the War-God!

We brought him to. He asked where he was wounded,
And insisted on paying ransom to the wall.

THE MISER AND THE MOUSE

Asklepiadês the miser, chancing one morning to meet
A mouse in his house, addressed it: 'My very dear Mouse,
Why are you here?'
                To whom, with the sweetest smile,
The mouse made courteous answer: 'My frugal friend,
Take heart! I expect no board from you:
                                only a bed.

TO LYKAINIS: A METAPHOR

Tell her this, Dorkas:
> *Meleagros to Lykainis:*
> *And so your kisses turn out to be counterfeit coin:*
> *Time's worn them down to the brass.*

ON LOT'S WIFE TURNED TO SALT

This is a tomb, no corpse within;
This is a corpse, no tomb without:
Corpse-shell self-tombed, self in self.

DEPOSITION

I despise yr interminable novels-in-verse
Yr well travelled highways please me not
I abominate yr ubiquitous back-slappers
I will not drink from the common spring
&
I abhor anything popular.

THE SIDON GIRLS! THE SIDON GIRLS!

O scaly-backed Lykainis,
O shame of Aphroditê,
Lykainis, shapeless as a starved snake,
Lykainis, from whose bed
The lousiest drunken goatherd would bolt in horror:
Yah! Yah!
These are the girls you meet in Sidon!

EPITAPH OF NEARCHOS

Rest lightly O Earth upon this wretched Nearchos
That the dogs may have no trouble in dragging him out.

MEDITATION

Praise, of course, is best: plain speech breeds hate.
But ah the Attic honey
Of telling a man exactly what you think of him!

INSCRIPTION FOR A SMYRNA PRIVY

And so your head aches, friend? and so
Your heavy body groans with sluggishness,
And you must knead your paunch with both hands to dis-
   lodge
The delicious work of your jaws?
What a fool!
Then was the time to think of it when you lay,
Most hog-like, gorging at table, in love with your own
Capacity.
And so, well may you sit here now:
The latter end of all your delight is this,
That you pummel your belly for the sins your throat com-
   mitted.

THE SOBER COMPANION

More than the Pleiadês' setting
More than the yammering surf at the point of the jetty
More than the frenzied lightning that scores the vast arch
   of the sky
I fear the man who drinks water
And so remembers this morning what the rest of us said
   last night.

PARADOX

This man: this no-thing: vile: this brutish slave:
This man is beloved, and rules another's soul.

EPITAPH OF A SLAVE

Alive, this man was Manês the slave: but dead,
He is the peer of Dareios, that great King.

EPITAPH OF A SAILOR

Tomorrow the wind will have fallen
Tomorrow I shall be safe in harbour
Tomorrow
      I said:
         and Death
Spoke in that little word:
The sea was Death.
      O Stranger
This is the Némesis of the spoken word:
Bite back the daring tongue that would say
  Tomorrow!

ANONYMOUS

EPITAPH OF A YOUNG MAN

Hail me Diogenês underground, O Stranger, and pass by:
Go where you will, and fairest fortune go with you.
In my nineteenth year the darkness drew me down—

And ah, the sweet sun!

KALLIMACHOS

EPITAPH OF A YOUNG CHILD

His father Philip laid here the twelve-year-old boy
    Nikotelês:
        his dearest hope.

THEODORIDAS OF SYRACUSE

EPITAPH OF A SAILOR

I am the tomb of a mariner shipwrecked.
Sail on:
Even while we died the others rode out the storm.

EPITAPH OF A SAILOR

And Thymodês also, lamenting a death unforeseen,
Raised up this empty tomb for Lykos his son:

For him there is no grave, not even in a far land:
Some Thynian beach or Pontine island holds him,

And there, cheated of all the rites of burial,
His bones gleam naked on an unfriendly shore.

EPITAPH OF A BOY

Look on this tomb of a dead boy,
                    Kleoitês the son of Menesaichmos,
And pity him, Stranger, who was beautiful, and who died.

EPITAPH OF A SAILOR

These were my end: a fierce down-squall from the east,
And night, and the waves of Orion's stormy setting:
And I, Kallaischros, yielded my life
Far on the waste of the lonely Libyan sea.

And now I roll with drifting currents, the prey
Of fishes:
           and this gravestone lies
If it says that it marks the place of my burial.

ANONYMOUS

EPITAPH OF A DOG

Stranger by the roadside, do not smile
When you see this grave, though it is only a dog's.
My master wept when I died, and his own hand
Laid me in earth and wrote these lines on my tomb.

EPITAPH OF A COURTESAN

Here lies Archeanassa of Kolophôn, whose face
Even when scored by age was sweet Love's throne.
Ah lovers, lovers,
You of her young days, gathering those flowers
In their first beauty,

through what a fire you passed!

LEONIDAS OF TARENTUM

EPITAPH OF AN ABSTAINER

Remember Euboulos the sober, you who pass by,
And drink: there is one Hadês for all men.

PLATO

ON THE ERETRIAN EXILES

Who left long ago the Aigaian's shattering surge,
Now lie we here
In mid-plain Ekbátana. Farewell to famous
Eretria, once our country! Farewell Athens
Near to Euboia!

and fare well, dear sea!

E   *65*

EPITAPH OF CHARIDAS OF KYRENE

And does Charidas sleep there in death, O Stone, beneath
   thee?
If you speak of Arimmas' son of Kyrênê, beneath me.

O Charidas, what of the world below?—*A great Dark.*
O Charidas, what of resurrection?—*A lie.*
O Charidas, what of Pluto?—

                      The ghost of a ghost :
We die for ever.

KRINAGORAS

SEPULCHRAL IMPRECATION

Here lies Eunikidês. The tomb
Weighs hard on him, grinds down his hated head,
The cracked foul teeth, bursts
His pouting breast, his legs swollen with gyves,
And the scraped skull green with the slime of rotted flesh.

O Earth, in this strange bridal
Lie not light on the filth of your monstrous groom.

EPITAPH

For Pythonax and his brother, locked away
In earth before the noontide of their youth,
Megaristos their father raises
This stone,
        a deathless gift to his sons deathbound.

THEON OF ALEXANDRIA

FOR THE CENOTAPH OF A LOST SAILOR

You are the charge of halcyons now, it may be:
But—oh Lenaios!—your mother
Bends in still anguish above your empty tomb.

ANONYMOUS

EPITAPH OF EPIKTETOS

I was a slave: crippled in body:
Poor as Iros:
        and loved by the gods.

EPITAPH OF A THESSALIAN HOUND

Surely I think the wild beasts fear your white bones
Even though you lie here dead, Lykas, brave huntress!
Your valour great Pêlion knows,
                                    and mighty Ossa,
And the wind-swept lonely ways of high Kithairon.

EPITAPH OF A MALTESE WATCH-DOG

Beneath me (says the stone) lies the white dog from Melita,
The faithful sentinel of Eumêlos' house:
                                    living,
His name was Bully Boy; but now, in death,
His barking is hushed in the empty ways of night.

EPITAPH OF A PET HARE

Light-footed, floppy-eared,
The baby hare:
Snatched away from my mother to be the pet
Of sweet-skinned Phanion:
                    Spring blossoms
Were all my food,
                    my mother was soon forgotten:
But I died at last of surfeit of dewy petals!
Now beside her bed my mistress has made my grave,
Even in dreams to keep me close to her breast.

A GENERAL EPITAPH

My name is—What does it matter?—*My
Country was*—Why speak of it?—*I
Was of noble birth*—Indeed? And if
You had been of the lowest?—*Moreover, my life
Was decorous*—And if it had not been so,
What then?
                    —*and I lie here now beneath you*—

Who are you that speak?
To whom do you speak?

69

AT THE TOMB OF SOPHOKLES

Gently about this tomb wind gently O Ivy
where Sophoklês lies

                  mingle your green with the rose
and the new tendrils of the gathering vine
soft-cluster

            For his sake whose dark wise heart
shuddered with the glory of the Deathless Ones
who spoke through his fatal tongue.

ELEGY ON HERAKLEITOS

One brought me the news of your death, O Herakleitos
   my friend,
And I wept for you, remembering
How often we had watched the sun set as we talked.

And you are ashes now, old friend from Halikarnassos,
Ashes now:

            but your nightingale songs live on,
And Death, the destroyer of every lovely thing,
Shall not touch them with his blind all-cancelling fingers.

ELEGY ON HIS FRIEND DION,
TYRANT OF SYRACUSE

Tears were for Hekabê, friend, and for Ilion's women,
Spun into the dark Web on the day of their birth,
But for you our hopes were great, and great the triumph,
Cancelled alike by the gods at the point of glory.
Now you lie in your own land, now all men honour you—

But I loved you, O Diôn!

PTOLEMAIOS THE ASTRONOMER

STAR-GAZING

That I am mortal I know and do confess
My span of a day:
                    but when I gaze upon
The thousandfold circling gyre of the stars,
No longer do I walk on earth
                              but rise
The peer of God himself to take my fill
At the ambrosial banquet of the Undying.

'THE LYF SO SHORT'

But the brief pleasures of life! but the
Headlong fugue of time passing!
                              Waking,
Sleeping, playing, contriving, with Time against us,
Marching always against us, swerving us
To our end—
        and that's nothing.

THEOGNIS

GNOMIC VERSES

The best of all things it were, never to be born,
Never to know the light of the strong sharp sun;
But being born,
The best of all is to pass as soon as may be
To Hadês' gate,
                there to lie dead,
Lost, locked close beneath the world's huge weight.

TIMON THE MISANTHROPE

Timôn, since you are dead,
Which do you hate more, the darkness or the light?
The darkness, man:
> *there are more of you here in Hell.*

INSCRIPTION FOR THE TOMB OF TIMON

Ask neither my name nor my country, passers-by:
My sole wish is that all of you may die.

MODUS VIVENDI

In silence walk your wretched span; in silence
Be like Time, that passes silently.
And live unheeded:
> you shall be so, once dead.

'NOBIS CUM SEMEL OCCIDIT BREVIS LUX'

Drink down the strong wine: Dawn's but the span of a
    finger,
And shall we wait for the lamp that brings *Good night*?
Drink, drink to joy, dear friend:

                          for soon we'll have
A lonely night for sleeping, and that's for ever.

'PLATO'S ELYSIUM'

Crying *Farewell O Sun!*, Kleombrotos of Ambrakia
Leaped down to Hadês from a high wall:
Driven by no evil
To suicide, but only that he had read
Plato's one mighty treatise on the Soul.

'MEMENTO HOMO QUIA PULVIS ES'

O Man consider how thy father sowed thee:
Think, and all thy vanity shall fall from thee.
Was it not Plato's dreaming
Begot the pride that hails thee 'deathless', 'divine'?
Or one has told thee
Remember O Man that thou art dust, and be humble!
So the sonorous line.
                    But hear this,
My ruder Truth: *Thou art born of Lust unchained*
And most vile Flux.

PRAYER BEFORE DEATH

My nurse was the island of Tyre: the land of my birth
Was Attic land, Syrian Gádara: I sprang
From Eukratês' stock: I Meleagros: friend of the Muses:
Quickest of those to be swayed by the wit of Menippos.
And a Syrian:
                but the world, Stranger,
Is one country to us all: of one Chaos
Were all men born.
                    And now
Stricken with age I have made this poem before burial,
Remembering that old men share their houses with Death.
But you, wish me well, the old man rambling in speech,
And so attain yourself to a chattering old age.

75

MELEAGROS

HIS EPITAPH

Quietly O Stranger pass by:
>   here sleeps an old man
Cradled with the holy dead in the common silence:
Meleagros: Eukratês' son: who joined in song
Sweetcrying Love with the Muses and smiling Graces.
Him divine Tyre and Gádara's sacred land
Sheltered till manhood: but his old age was nursed
By lovely Kôs of the Meropês.
>   And now O friend
Shálam if you are a Syrian:
>   if Phoinikian, *Naidios*:
But if Greek, *Fare well!*
>   and give me back the same.

JULIANUS AEGYPTIUS

THE TOMB OF ANAKREON

I have sung this often,
>   even in the grave will I shout it:
Drink: for you must put on this mantle of dust.